LEIF ERIKSSON

BY SHANNON KNUDSEN

ILLUSTRATIONS BY MARK OLDROYD

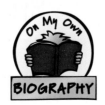

On My Own

BIOGRAPHY

🌿 Carolrhoda Books, Inc./Minneapolis

For those who brave the unknown in search of a better life
—S.K.

To George and Jesse, my little Vikings
—M.O.

This book is available in two editions:
Library binding by Carolrhoda Books, Inc., a division of Lerner Publishing Group
Soft cover by First Avenue Editions, an imprint of Lerner Publishing Group
241 First Avenue North
Minneapolis, MN 55401 U.S.A.

Website address: www.carolrhodabooks.com

Library of Congress Cataloging-in-Publication Data

Knudsen, Shannon, 1971–
    Leif Eriksson / by Shannon Knudsen ; illustrations by Mark Oldroyd.
        p.   cm. — (On my own biography)
    ISBN: 1–57505–649–6 (lib. bdg. : alk. paper)
    ISBN: 1–57505–828–6 (pbk. : alk. paper)
    1. Leif Eriksson, d. ca. 1020—Juvenile literature. 2. Explorers—America—Biography—Juvenile literature. 3. Explorers—Scandinavia—Biography—Juvenile literature. 4. America—Discovery and exploration—Norse—Juvenile literature. 5. Vikings—Juvenile literature. I. Oldroyd, Mark, ill. II. Title. III. Series.
    E105.L47K59 2005
    970.01'3'092—dc22   2004002960

Manufactured in the United States of America
1 2 3 4 5 6 – DP – 10 09 08 07 06 05

Author's Note

Many people think that Christopher Columbus was the first European to come to America. Columbus crossed the Atlantic Ocean to reach America in 1492. His journey led other Europeans to sail there too. Over time, Europeans built settlements in America. The settlers fought wars with Native Americans and with each other. We remember Columbus because his travels led to these important changes. But he was not the first person from Europe to set foot in America.

Five hundred years before Columbus, a bold young man named Leif Eriksson sailed to North America. Leif was born in Iceland, an island of northern Europe. His people were skilled sailors and shipbuilders called Vikings. Leif wanted to find new land for the Vikings. He set out from the island of Greenland in an open boat, ready to brave the stormy Atlantic Ocean in search of the unknown. This is his story.

CRASH!
Huge waves hammered the Viking ship.
A small boy named Leif Eriksson
stared out over the water.
Where was Greenland, the land
his father had told him about?
Leif was leaving his home in Iceland
for a new life there.

Leif's father was called Erik the Red.
He had red hair and a red-hot temper too.
Three years before, Erik had
killed two men in Iceland.
Because of these killings, he was
ordered to leave Iceland.

Erik sailed west to Greenland.
He explored the land
and decided to settle there.
He gathered many Vikings
to build a settlement
in the year 985.
He brought his wife
and his son, Leif.

When the Vikings reached
Greenland, they built homes.
Erik the Red became an important
leader called a chieftain.
He worked hard to help the settlers
find food and make decisions.
Erik was often busy.
So Leif spent a lot of time
with his foster father,
a German man named Tyrkir.

As Leif grew up, he worked hard,
just as his father did.
He learned to hunt and fish for food.
He learned to handle a boat
and chop down ripe grain
with a knife.

One day, Leif heard an amazing story.
It was about a man
named Bjarni Herjolfsson.
Years before, in 986,
Bjarni had gone on a trip
from Iceland to Greenland.
On the way, fog surrounded his ship.
Soon the ship was lost.
After days of sailing,
Bjarni came to three lands
that no other Viking had seen.

The first place had hills and forests.
Next, he saw a flat land with trees.
The third land was also flat.
It was covered with huge blocks
of ice called glaciers.
At last, Bjarni and his crew
found their way to Greenland.
Everyone was amazed to hear
where Bjarni had been.
Could the places Bjarni
talked about be real?

A Daring Journey
about the year 1000

Years went by.
Leif grew into a tall,
strong young man.
He never forgot the story
of Bjarni's discoveries.
What would life be like in the
mystery lands to the west?
A journey to the west
would be dangerous.
Ocean storms could sink a ship.
Some people said that horrible
monsters lived across the ocean.

But Greenland was getting crowded.

People needed new places to live.

To the east, the land was already settled.

West was the best way to go
to find new homes.

At last, Leif made up his mind.

He would find the lands Bjarni had seen.

Leif bought Bjarni's ship.

Bjarni told Leif which way to sail.

Next, Leif gathered a crew of 35 men.

Some of them had sailed with Bjarni.

They would help Leif find the way.

His father, Erik, would come too.

So would Tyrkir, the foster father

who had helped raise Leif.

Leif made sure the ship was strong.

The boards fit together tightly to keep out water.

The thick woolen sail would catch

the wind to move the ship along.

One man could row in the ship's front.

Another man could row in the back.

A wooden part called a rudder

could be moved to steer the ship.

The time came for Leif

and the crew to set sail.

But something went wrong.

On his way to the ship,

Erik fell from his horse.

He hurt his leg badly.

How could he make the hard trip ahead?

Erik saw that his days as an
explorer were behind him.
"This is as far as we go
together," he told Leif.
Father and son parted at the shore.
Leif would have to make his way
without his father's help.

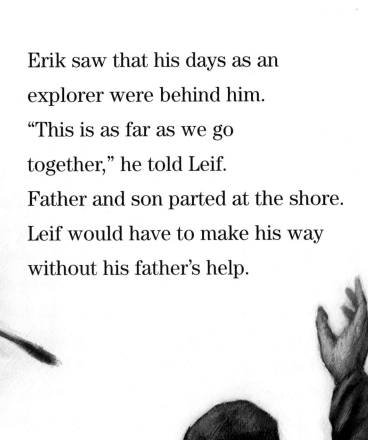

Across the Ocean

The crew set sail
on the Atlantic Ocean.
For a few days, Leif sailed along
the coast of Greenland.
He kept the land in sight.
That way, he wouldn't get lost
on the huge ocean.
But finally he had to turn his ship
away from the land.

Leif watched the sun during the day.

He watched the stars at night.

The movements of the sun
and stars told him which way
the ship was going.

The ship did not get lost.

Still, the sailing wasn't easy.
Wind and rain made it
hard to stay dry.

Waves splashed into the open boat.
The men scooped the water out
when it got too deep.

23

After a few days,

the sailors spotted land.

Leif ordered them to drop the anchor.

They used a small boat to row to shore.

This land looked just like the

third land that Bjarni had seen.

It was a huge, flat slab of rock.

Icy glaciers covered much of the rock.
No grass grew for farm animals to eat.
Leif told his crew that
the land was not good.
He named it Helluland.
This name means stone-slab land.

The crew rowed back to the ship.
They sailed south across the water
until they found land again.
Leif saw that this land looked like
the second land Bjarni had found.
It had beautiful beaches of white sand.
Forests of tall trees stretched
as far as Leif could see.

But there was no grass for animals to eat.
Leif named this land Markland,
which means forest land.

The explorers sailed on for two more days.

Early one morning, they
rowed to an island.

At last, Leif saw the grass
he had been looking for.

It was wet with drops of morning dew.

The men drank the dew
with their hands.
They had gone many days
without fresh water.
The dew was the sweetest thing
they had ever tasted.

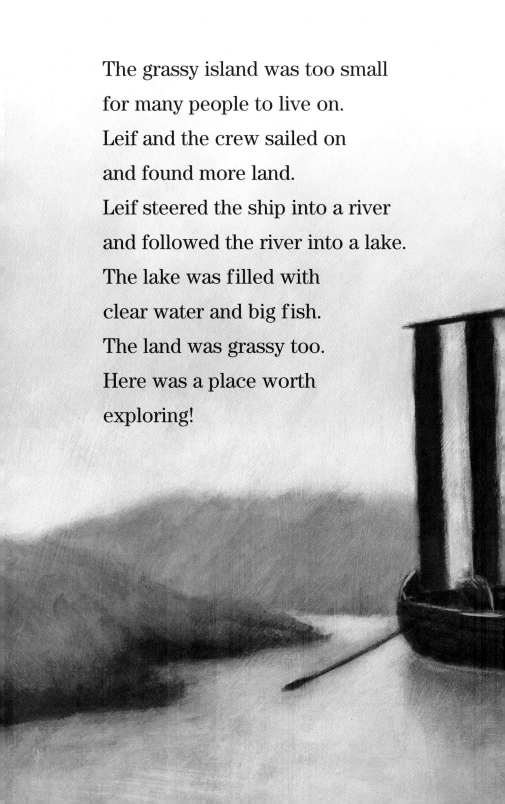

The grassy island was too small
for many people to live on.
Leif and the crew sailed on
and found more land.
Leif steered the ship into a river
and followed the river into a lake.
The lake was filled with
clear water and big fish.
The land was grassy too.
Here was a place worth
exploring!

Land of Grapes and Wood

Before the men could explore safely,
they needed shelter.
Leif and his men went to work.
They cut thick chunks of grassy earth
and stacked them to build houses.
Then they wove together
branches to make roofs.
The finished houses were called booths.

The land seemed good to Leif.
The weather was warmer
than it was in Greenland.
Daytime lasted longer too.
Leif decided to spend the winter.
He and his crew built better
houses with thick walls,
strong roofs, and fireplaces.

Each day, Leif sent half the crew
to explore the land.
Sometimes he went with them.
Other times, he worked with
the rest of the crew.
The explorers met no people.

But they found beautiful forests
and plenty of animals to hunt.
One night, one of the men did not
come back from exploring.
It was Tyrkir, Leif's foster father.
Where could he be?

Leif took 12 men to search for Tyrkir.
They had just started looking
when Tyrkir came back.
He was safe!
He had explored farther than
the men had ever gone.
To the south, he found grapes
growing on vines.
This was wonderful news.
Grapes could be made into wine.
And wine could be traded
for money and goods.

Leif and the crew went to work again.

They cut down grapevines

and picked the grapes.

They cut down trees too.

Wood was hard to find back in Greenland.

These trees could be used to build boats.

The crew filled Leif's ship and the rowboat

with wood and grapes.

Winter passed, and spring came.

It was time to go home.

As the men set sail,

Leif named the land.

He called it Vinland,

which means wine land.

Leif the Lucky

The winds blew the ship and crew
straight home to Greenland.
When they were almost home,
Leif spotted a rocky reef
poking out of the water ahead.

He thought he could see
people on the reef too.
Leif sailed to the reef.
Sure enough, 15 people
shouted and waved.
Their ship had hit the reef and sunk.
They had been stranded.
If Leif's ship hadn't come along,
they would have died.

Leif welcomed his new passengers.
With a ship full of friends and crew,
grapes and wood, he sailed home.
At last, he saw his father again.
He told everyone the story of Vinland.
People couldn't hear enough
about his adventures.

He became famous in all
the Viking lands for the places
and things he had found.
From then on, Leif Eriksson
had a new name.
He was known as Leif the Lucky.

Afterword

Leif never returned to the land he named Vinland. His father died soon after Leif came back to Greenland. Leif had to take over as the leader of the Greenland settlement. But other Vikings, including Leif's brother and sister, followed his example and visited Vinland. They explored the land and met Native Americans. The Native Americans fought to protect their homeland. In about 1015, the Vikings left Vinland. They returned for short visits to look for wood, but they never settled again in North America.

For many years, people who study the past weren't sure about parts of Leif's story. He didn't leave behind a map of his travels. Was his story true? If so, where were the places he called Helluland, Markland, and Vinland?

In 1961, the remains of Viking houses were found in Newfoundland, Canada. Most people agree that Newfoundland is probably Vinland, the place where Leif and his crew built houses. Helluland and Markland are probably parts of Canada that are north of Newfoundland. We may never know the whole story of Leif Eriksson's adventures. But we do know that his daring journey was the first time a European set foot in America.

Important Dates

Some of the important dates of Leif Eriksson's
life are not known for certain.

about 980—Leif Eriksson (LEEF AYR-ihk-suhn) is born
 in Iceland.
982—Leif's father, Erik the Red, is ordered to leave Iceland.
 Erik spends the next three years exploring Greenland.
985—Leif moves with his family to Greenland.
986—Bjarni Herjolfsson (bih-YAHR-nee hayr-YOHLF-suhn)
 sails past unknown lands to the west of Iceland.
about 998—Some stories say that Leif's son is born at
 this time.
about 1000—Leif and his crew sail to North America and
 spend the winter there.
about 1001—Leif and his crew return to Greenland.
about 1025—Leif dies in Greenland.

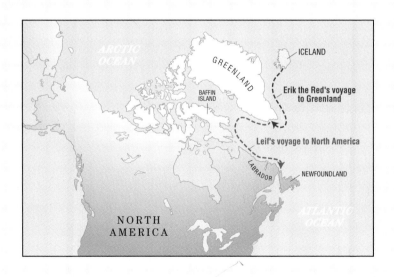